The Book of Why?

Kimberley Dawn McAninch

The Book of Why?

tellwell

Tellwell Talent
www.tellwell.ca

ISBN
978-0-2288-3820-3 (Hardcover)
978-0-2288-2847-1 (Paperback)
978-0-2288-2848-8 (eBook)

Dedicated to all teachers and parents who are asked this question on a daily basis to help our children better understand the world around us.

Why?

Why? We ask this question every day because it helps us understand the world better.

Why do killer whales travel in pods?
Hmm... I'm not sure. Lets check it out!

The question *Why* encourages us to question the way things are in this moment. By teaching students to ask questions starting with the word *Why*, we can change a child's point of view or perspective about something they are curious about. Their understanding will deepen as a result.

Possible teacher prompt: We have been learning about sea creatures and their habitats. Turn to a partner and create a question beginning with the word *Why* to help you learn more about your inquiry. This *Why* question may lead your inquiry into a whole new direction!

WhY?

What a powerful word!

Why are dinosaurs extinct?
WHY?
Why does t
earth rota
around the
sun?

This word can impact our lives in so many ways. *Why* makes us think about what we want to learn more about. Now, that's something to think about!

WHY DO animals HAVE CAMOUFLAGE?
PROTECT THEM FROM

Why is such a unique word because it invites the learning of something new! That's remarkable!

The word *Why* makes us think more deeply and thoughtfully about the world around us.

Why do people have so many gifts and talents?

Why is such an amazing word because it helps us start conversations and build knowledge about something new!

WHY?
is important because

Why is *Why* so important?

Why creates so many awesome questions!

Why does an octopus have eight legs?

Why does the moon rotate around the Earth?

Why is it important to eat healthy foods?

Why is the sky blue?

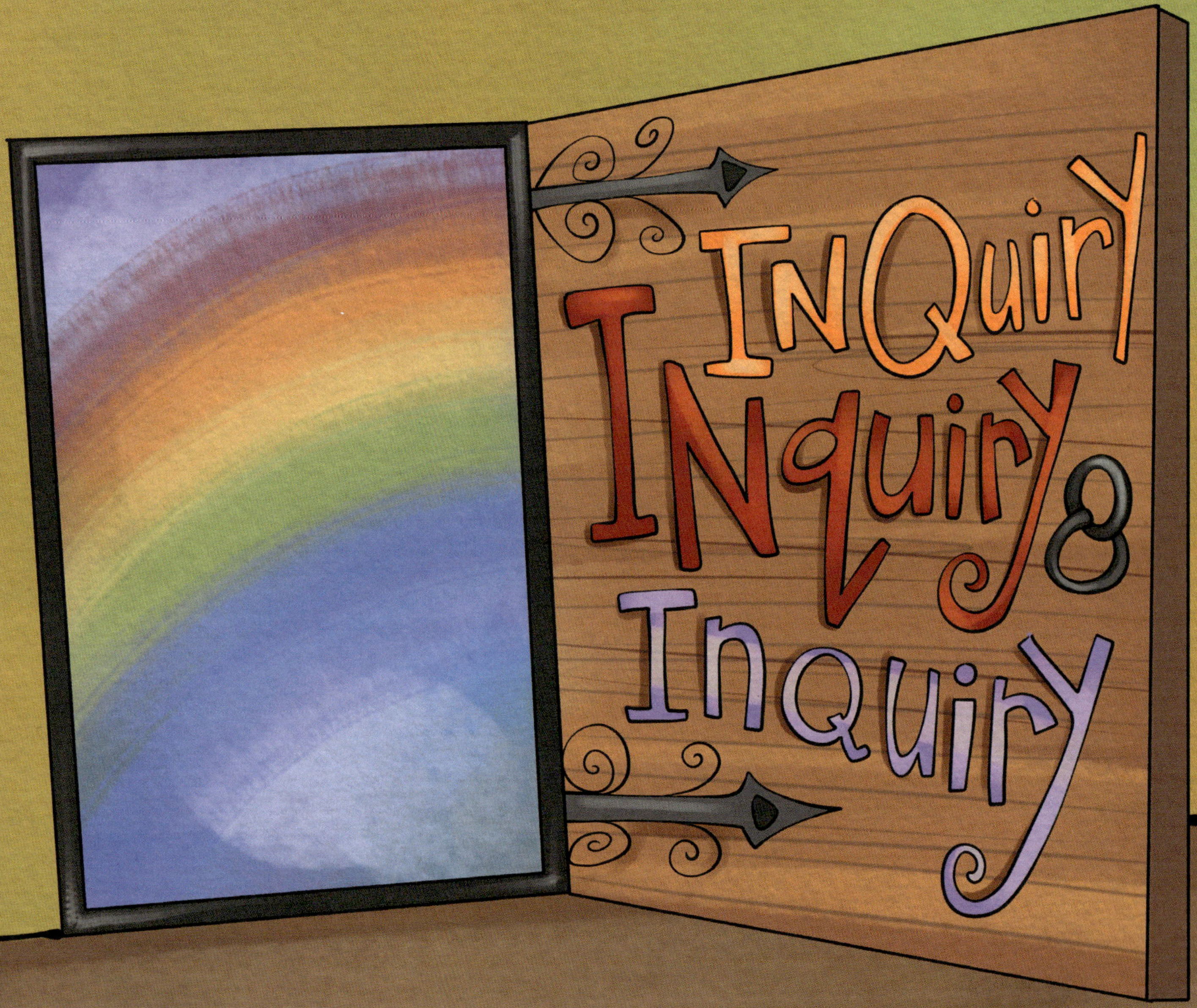
Inquiry
Inquiry &
Inquiry

Why opens the door to inquiry. What is inquiry, you ask? That is a topic for another book.

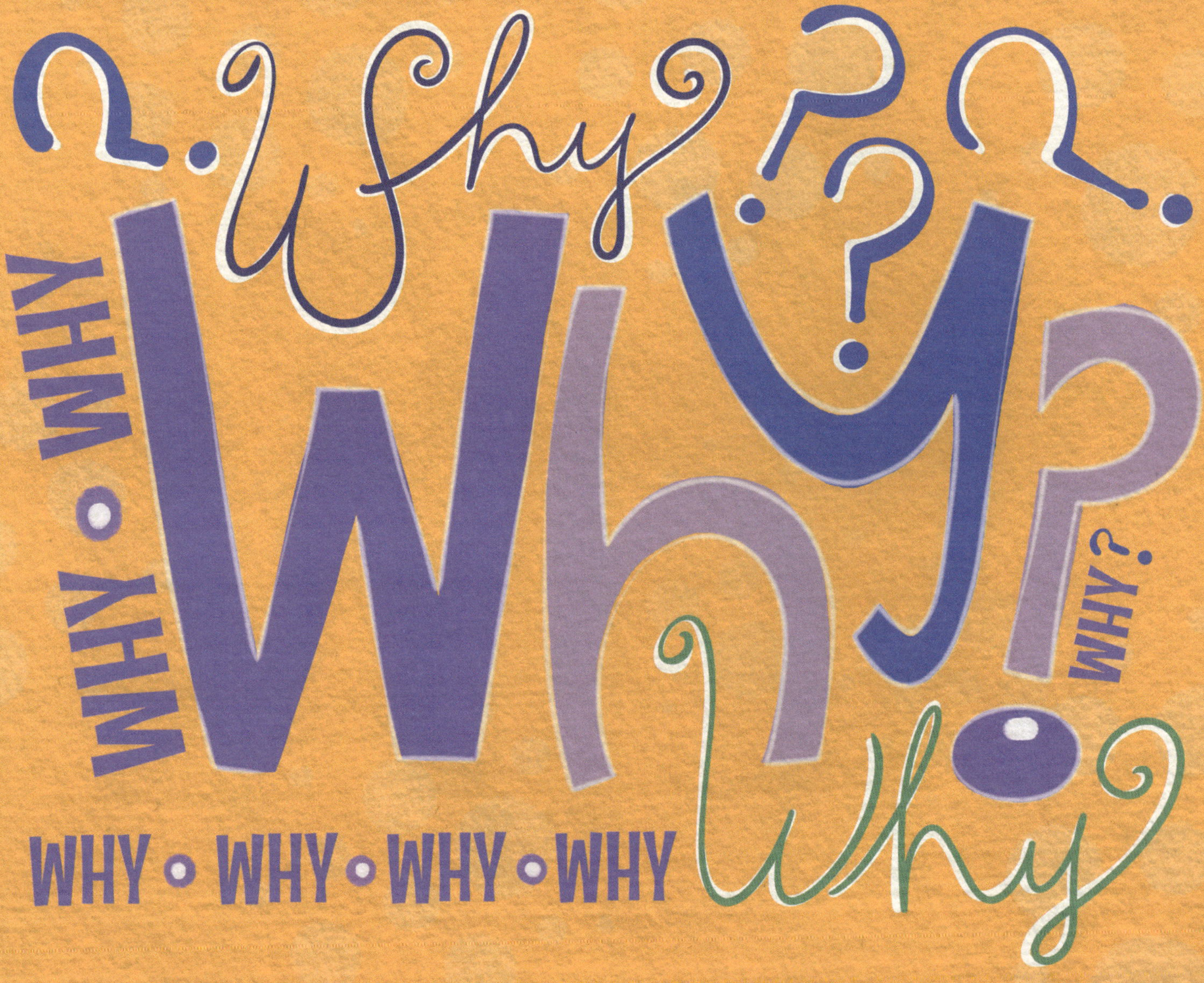
Why?
Why?
WHY • WHY
WHY?
WHY • WHY • WHY • WHY
Why?

Ask your own awesome *Why* questions.

1.

2.

3.

4.

5.

SUPER!
AMAZING!
Marvelous!
EXCELLENT!
SUPER